A HUGE THANK YOU TO EVERYONE WHO CONTRIBUTED TO THIS BOOK BY PROVIDING YOUR CREATIVE RESPONSES AND PHOTOGRAPHS. WITH YOUR SUPPORT AND ENTHUSIASM MY VISION CAME TO LIFE. I AM SO GRATEFUL TO BE A PART OF THIS COMMUNITY.

— XO JANNE

ISBN-13: 9780692548608
ISBN-10: 0692548602

Designed by Sky Roach, SKY DESIGN

Edited by Jennie Lay

Front and back cover photographs by Austin Colbert

My Three Girls Publishing
PO Box 880130
Steamboat Springs, CO 80488

www.deartaffy.com

PROLOGUE

Animals are a true gift of love to us. They teach us the meaning of unconditional love, living in the moment and living simply. My own pets mean the world to me and fill me with immeasurable joy. They make me happy when I'm down, smile when I want to cry or remain steady when silence is needed. For pet lovers, it is heartbreaking to witness the number of pets who don't have a "forever home." Usually, this is through no fault of their own, and these pets spend their days in shelters, waiting and hoping for someone upon whom they can bestow their love.

The Steamboat Springs animal shelter, managed by the Routt County Humane Society (RCHS), does a phenomenal job with the animals that come through its care, providing love, attention, veterinary care and promotion to help place each animal in a forever home. Knowing how much vibrant positive energy our pets bring into our home, I wanted to bring this book to life and give pets who are lucky to have found their families an opportunity to give back, tell their stories and give a voice to those pets who are still searching. As such, the idea behind this book is to have pets in forever homes (some of who came from the shelter themselves) tell the stories of their daily lives, share their life philosophies, and offer advice to both pets going into a new home and families who are bringing a new pet into their home.

It is my hope that through the eyes, wisdom and love of our pets, this book will generate a substantial profit to help RCHS make life better for animals awaiting their forever homes, as a portion of the book proceeds will go to RCHS to offset new expenses and improvements at the Steamboat Springs shelter. Regardless of where you live, the unique words of wisdom and stories from these pets will make you smile, laugh and cry.

IN ADDITION TO THIS BOOK, I INVITE YOU TO VISIT MY BLOG, DEARTAFFY.COM, and fill out a questionnaire for your pet or submit a question and see what other pets have to say about life, love, food and the value of napping. Thank you for your purchase of this book and your support of RCHS.

INTRODUCTION

TAFFY: We've never written a book before, but when Mom asked us (mostly me, really) to write this part, we agreed to help her. I am Taffy Siegel, a brilliant and talented Border Collie. Assisting me is my little sister, Astin, an annoying Australian Shepard. You will read more about me later in this book.

ASTIN: I am not just an assistant, Taffy and I'm not annoying. Mom said we BOTH write equal parts. You are not always the boss. And besides, Mom will know if you are a book hog. And I am featured in this book, too!

TAFFY: Okay, whatever. Anyway, Mom has had this idea for over two years to write a book from a pet's point of view. Of course, it is a brilliant idea. Pets are insightful, smart, loyal, live in the moment, present in our lives and love our families unconditionally. Astin and I know we (and our friends) are lucky to live in Steamboat Springs. We have warm beds at night, full bowls of food, water and lots of yummy treats. We play in the snow all winter, and hike on the trails and swim in the Yampa River during the summer.

Did we mention the treats and snacks?

Unfortunately, Mom knows about some pets who live in our county (Astin doesn't even know what a "county" is....) who are not so fortunate. They are looking for their forever homes.

ASTIN: I do too know what a county is! Mom explained the difference between a city and county to me. Mom also told me that the Routt County Humane Society is the organization (and I know what that is too) that helps pets find a forever home, and also takes care of pets who are still looking for that special place. Mom said if she could, she would bring all of the waiting pets home with her. (Although that would be awkward. Just sayin'.) Mom also knows how much love, companionship and happiness us pets (and I use that term loosely – we all know we are virtually human) bring to our families.

6

MY TURN. TAFFY HERE. So (I don't know whether you can actually start a sentence with "So" but I am pretty sure I can. Mom will tell me), Mom thought and thought about what she could do to help Routt County Humane Society that would be fun and different. Knowing that Steamboat is such a pet friendly – almost pet crazy – community, she thought it would be nice for pets who live the good life to help those less fortunate. She compiled a list of questions she thought would be fun to ask us pets.

ASTIN: You had a full paragraph there, Taffy. So (I know you can start a sentence with "So" – it is known as a discourse marker), Taffy and I suggested that we, with Mom's help, interview our furry friends. We sent questions to pet owners and lovers around Routt County and all those Moms, Dads and family members were great translators, asking their pets our questions and returning responses along with a picture or two. Then we put everyone's stories together to create this book.

TAFFY: Of course, Astin forgot to mention the best part of the whole project: a percentage of the net proceeds from this book will go directly to Routt County Humane Society to help them fund their programs! Mom will tell you more about that later in this book. I think Mom had fun writing this book, even though we would see her get out of her chair a zillion times some days. (Yes, that is a real number and Astin has no idea how many zeros are in a zillion.) We actually liked those days because we usually got a treat every time she got up.

But I digress.

TAFFY: I know Mom wants to thank all of the pets who shared their stories with us. Mom would also like to thank the Routt County Humane Society board members who patiently and tirelessly answered her thousands of questions and provided the organizational information (big words for most pets, but not a Border Collie) Mom put in the book. I am also sure Mom wants to thank our family for all of their love and support, and especially us (mostly me), who sat at her feet while she wrote.

ASTIN: Just so you know she wants to thank Dad mostly (that is an adverb). He read drafts, gave her encouragement when she doubted, and always believed in her and this project. Also, she wants to thank Lauren and Ben who each wrote a part in this book (not as big as ours, but still, a part). She is very grateful to Schuyler Roach, who designed and formatted this beautiful book, and to Jennie Lay, who helped her edit and bring this book to life.

TAFFY: Okay, enough already, Astin. Let's move on and read what our furry friends have to say about life, love, food and snacks, plus all the advice they have for new pets and new owners.

BUDDY

What do you do when you are home alone?

I eat Mom's underwear. Dad says that because I do this he has some serious receipts stacked up from a place Mom calls Vicky's.

Do you like being an only pet?

Wait, they could have another? Why would anyone want another pet when they have me? I'm all they could ever want or need!!!

What is your favorite memory?

I escaped from Grandma and Grandpa's house and followed a hot blonde to the top of Storm Peak. Apparently, guys in red jackets with white crosses on them like me because they surrounded me with hot dogs and took me down the Gondola. It was such an excellent day that I went back up there again the next day.

What is your favorite treat?

Cookie...Cookie!?!? Where? I'm lying down, shake, yeah I'm shaking...where's the treat?!?!?! Come, stay, rollover... PLEASE give me a treat!!!!'

What annoys you the most?

When my parents pay more attention to their jobs than me.

"I WANT TO GET FAT. I DON'T KNOW WHAT THAT WORD MEANS, BUT I'M TOLD IF I KEEP EATING I WILL GET FAT, AND THAT SOUNDS GOOD. I LIKE FAT." – BUDDY LAMB

COOPER

"MY PHILOSOPHY OF LIFE IS TO BE **'FULL OF JOY'.** EVERYTHING I DO IS BASED ON JOY. SOMETIMES I MIGHT BE *a little bit naughty,* BUT I'M NOT TRYING TO MAKE ANYONE MAD... I'M JUST TRYING TO HAVE FUN! EVERYTHING I DO IS OUT OF PURE **JOY."**

— COOPER MATTOX

Cooper shared his thoughts and passed over the Rainbow Bridge in 2015 during the production of this book♡

What are your likes and dislikes?

I like LOTS of things! Mostly things that start with the letter P. My favorite toys are my Purple Pony and my Pink Pig! I LOVE pizza, popcorn and peanut-butter. I don't really like fruit or vegetables. I love my family and can't wait to see them when they come home!

What is your favorite season and why?

I love early summer, when it's not too hot out and there is water in the ditches along the path. I always run to the water, and right before jumping in, I turn and look at my mom, who is usually telling me to "Stop!," and then...I jump right in! I also love the first big snowstorm! I love playing ball in the snow because I don't get too hot and I can dive under the pile of snow and look for my ball! Winter is also great because when I get thirsty on my walks I can just take a bite of snow.

What is your favorite treat?

My favorite treats are popcorn and pizza crust. Hands down. Remember the letter "P" thing?

LEROY & FRED

"KEEP LIFE SIMPLE AND FOLLOW YOUR OWN PATH. NO NEED TO GROWL WHEN A SIMPLE SNARL WILL DO. NO NEED TO RUSH OVER WHEN YOU HEAR YOUR NAME CALLED. ENJOY SNACKING ON THE SUCCULENT GRASSES AND MOVE AT YOUR OWN PACE."
— FRED ZOLTANI

"LIVE IN THE MOMENT. THAT'S WHERE YOU ARE LIKELY TO FIND THE TREATS AND THE NECK SNUGGLES."
— LEROY ZOLTANI

What is your favorite pastime?

LEROY: Chewing bones as big as me and biting my sister all over her body, especially her ears when I get excited.

FRED: Neck snuggles. What is a neck snuggle? It is really the only way I know how to show affection. If you are sitting down, I jump up onto your lap and put my neck in your neck and get as close as possible. I know I'm not allowed to lick your face – I mean, I really want to lick your face, but I'm going to use every ounce of self-control in my body to stop myself from licking your face and just enjoy my favorite activity – neck snuggling!

What do you do when you are home alone?

FRED: We pretty much like to do the same things when we are home alone – sleep, chew plastic things, scratch at things, open bags and find things, any kinds of things, and spread them out all over the living room.

Are you a morning or afternoon pet?

LEROY: Definitely afternoon pet. I do have a small bladder so I have to force myself to get up in the morning for a quick pee – usually when my mom heads to work – but then it is back to bed for me.

FRED: I have to agree with Leroy on this one. I don't even want to get out of bed in the morning, but I'm forced out because someone is afraid I'll have a mid-morning accident.

"REST IS UNDERRATED. NO NEED
TO HURRY. UNLESS YOU WANT TO
RUN, RUN FAST. AND, IF YOU SEE
WATER, ENJOY IT... DRINK IT, LAY
IN IT, YOU KNOW WHEN LIFE GIVES
YOU WATER, GO SWIMMING."
                    —BERNIE COLEMAN

BERNIE

Opal Bernadette Francine Bacon Coleman-Nielson

Can you tell the reader a little bit about your unusual name?

Yes, I was given the name, Opal Bernadette Francine Bacon Coleman-Nielson. People always think I am a boy. Little do they know I am a actually a Spanish speaking dog named Mika. I guess when you are adopted THEY get to choose.

What is your favorite pastime?

Duh! Swimming, OMG, I love swimming! I also love chasing Mom and Dad on skis in the winter. Long walks and belly rubs are also great ways to spend time.

What is your favorite season and why?

Spring!! It smells so good. I get to be outside ALL day. I get to roll in stinky stinky stuff and then get a really nice massage bath. Once, I got this twice in one day. Did I mention I get to be outside? Also, swimming. I love swimming.

What is your favorite treat?
BACON! BACON! BACON!

I mean, it is my middle name. I don't get this often or really at all; so, I would have to say carrots, veggies, lots of "healthy" kitchen scraps, gluten free sweet potato treats (yes, I am a gluten free dog), and, well, I like treats and I am good with anything they give me except kale. Kale is gross. And I do love Frosty Paws and a Bully Stick! We could really write a whole chapter on my treat intake, but I won't bore you with all the details.

ALEIGH

Aleigh shared her thoughts and passed over the Rainbow Bridge in 2015 during the production of this book.

> "EAT,
>
> SLEEP,
>
> LOVE!"
> —ALEIGH GOLD

What are your likes and dislikes?

I like to sleep (preferably on someone's lap), sunbathe and beg for treats

Do you like being an only pet?

I have been an only pet for a couple of years now. I had a great mentor, a yellow lab named Lucky. He is in heaven now, so I am responsible for patrolling the yard to chase bears, foxes, porcupines, birds, chipmunks and other dogs away. I guess I've been pretty lucky that none of them have fought back!

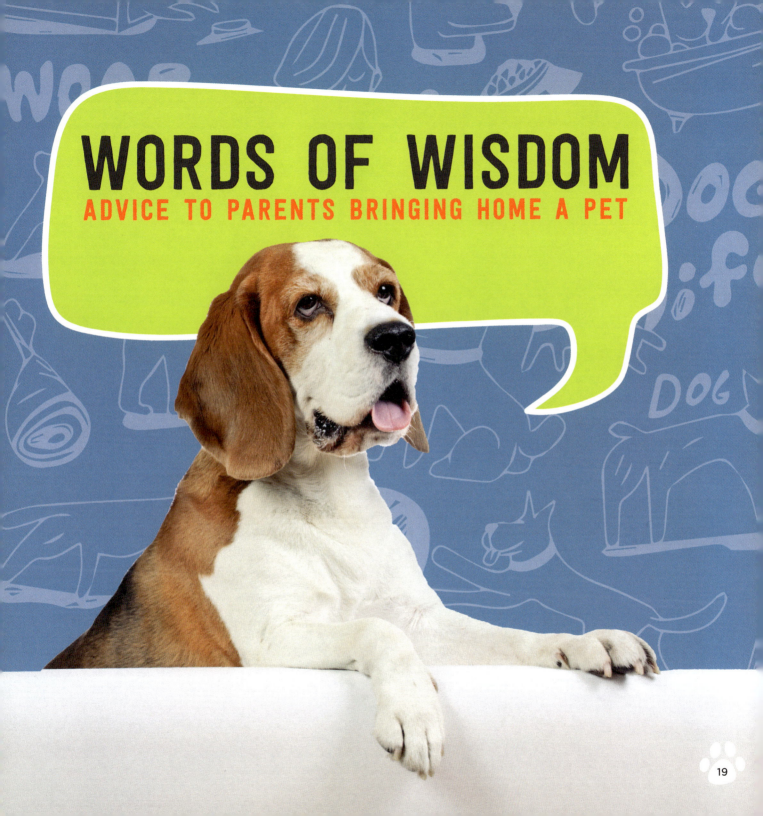

WORDS OF WISDOM
ADVICE TO PARENTS BRINGING HOME A PET

CLYDE SCROBBLE

Make sure you tell them you love them every day, like my best friend does with me.

BERNIE COLEMAN

My parents struggled with my name. Please name your pet a simple name, and do it on the first day. As for rules, all rules are flexible. Please see our NO DOGS in the bed policy.

ALEIGH GOLD

Remember that adopting a dog is a lifelong commitment. We are not disposable!

Alma Rose McKinley

Remember that new pets don't know what your rules are. Please have patience with your new pet and teach them as you would teach a child. Also, don't ever bring home a pet until you are really ready for one. Pets are not disposable. When you bring them home, that is a life-long commitment. They will give you unconditional love. Are you willing to do the same? Also, please remember that we have to go to the bathroom regularly (eight hours left alone is very difficult). Please don't leave us alone in a car in temperatures above 60 degrees, as we can overheat. We need water and food (different flavors and textures please - eating the same food day after day is not fun) and treats and lots and lots of love. And even if you have a back yard, we like to explore and sniff and go new places. We should be walked at least twice a day and have off-leash running and playing time. We are a big commitment.

JAKE RUNDELL Always let your dog sleep with you.

COOPER MATTOX

Make your dog/cat a part of the family. Don't get a dog if you are going to just stick it in the garage the whole time. We like to be just like another family member. I'll do anything for a treat, so that is a good thing to have around: lots of treats. And don't get too frustrated with your pet at first. Just learn to laugh a lot. We just want to have FUN!

Taffy Emerson

Love your pet and he or she will love you. Teach him/her what is expected and your pet will do what it can to reach your expectations. We dogs will love our people no matter what, but we also want to be treated well and taken care of. After all, we're fur-people and part of the family.

ECKO BOMBERG

To all future pet owners, Aussies are great!!! We are loyal, sensitive, smart, athletic and loveable.

FLAVIAS BORDEN

We learn how to act from how you act. Don't freak out if you don't want us to freak out.

ROXY TRACY

LOVE is all you need. But treats and good kibble help too. Make your new pet part of your family, spend as much time as possible with them, teach them by positive example, and your life will never be the same in the very best of ways. Give lots of treats. And don't get too frustrated with your pet at first. Just learn to laugh a lot. We just want to have fun.

21

Puppy Lalive

Get ready for adventure and for some nuttiness. The bottom line is this: You are going to be one happy, loved, kissed, talked to in weird voices, bathed, scolded if you mark in the house, applauded when you learn a new trick, breaking rules at times and overall healthy pet!

Josie Rundell

If you have puppies, let the mommy dog pick the puppy that gets to stay (Needless to say Jake was not my first choice, I wanted to keep Sophie).

Henry Kirkpatrick

Give your pet a chance to adapt to its new surroundings. Don't freak out if they take a while to adapt. It can be a very stressful situation.

LOLA MADER

Dogs are good at reading body language, so relax and breathe a little! Getting a pet is exciting, so don't stress. It'll all be ok!

Isis McAtee

Just have cats. Plain and simple.

Honey Badger Echtermeyer

Pets are a commitment. Do the right thing and spend time with them. Their life revolves around you and they want to be with you. Taking walks is good for everyone. Remember, a tired dog is a happy dog.

TESSA KOCIK

Get a leash and get going. There is a lot to see out there!

POUDRE McCAULLEY

Really look at what you are getting into, and evaluate your lifestyle before you commit to something for its cuteness. Not everyone would be a good family for me. That leaves a lot of Border Collies looking like they are bad dogs, when they are just bored. You really have to think about that.

MELON SWEERS
Dog is man's best friend.

MANGO SWEERS
Big puppies grow into big dogs.

Taffy, Astin & Tory Siegel

Taffy: We love you no matter what, so love us no matter what. Cut us some slack in the beginning and make sure to take us on walks... And pet us all the time. And scratch our backs... Yes! Yes! Yes!

Astin: Be patient and teach us what you want us to do. We want to do the right thing and please you, so just tell us the rules.

Tory: We are so grateful to have a forever home and we want to make you happy, so just give us love, lots of pets and have patience with us.

KENAI BYE A pet may not be your whole life, but it will make your life whole.

23

"WHATEVER..."
— BOB CAT OGDEN

BOB

My name is Bob. Bob Cat.

Yes, I know, very original. I'm eight or so. Whatever. I think I was born under the sign of the rat. Whatever. I adopted my current family after being "dropped off" at the vet's for a few days while my first family was on vacation. They said they'd be back to pick me up soon. I guess they got busy. Whatever. After a few months someone called "A Foster" came to pick me up. A few days later, someone came by their house to look me over and offer me a permanent home, but by then I'd decided to stay with "The Fosters." Whatever. They fed me, and had another pet for me... "a dog" who matched my black and white coloring. I enjoyed controlling him for many years until recently, when he laid down and didn't get back up. Whatever. I must admit, I'm a little nicer to "The Fosters" now that my dog is gone. They seem to be a little sad, so I scratch at their legs and bite their feet a little more these days to let them know they can still find comfort in scratching me. Whatever.

BIJOU & FELIZ

"YIPPEE .... IT'S ANOTHER WONDERFUL DAY ... I CAN'T WAIT TO EXPERIENCE IT!"

— FELIZ HERD

What do you do when you are home alone?

BIJOU: Sleep. **FELIZ:** Sleep.

Is there a specific story you would like to share?

BIJOU: Well, you see, I was diagnosed with a brain tumor. Suddenly I started having seizures late at night and two medical people dashed to the vet's office to meet me. I was taken to Denver the next day for lots of tests and put on a bunch of different medications which kept getting re-adjusted. The specialist gave me two years, tops – but I survived for four and a half more years because the vets and Mom and Dad did everything they could to keep me healthy and happy. They used to call me their miracle dog. I certainly would not have lived so long if it weren't for the extraordinary effort on the part of everyone to keep me here. At one point they nearly gave up, but didn't. I'm glad, because I sure didn't want to leave and I'm so happy I got to stay as long as I did. I think that's a nice story which shows great love and determination on everyone's part.

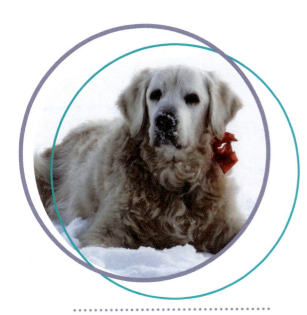

"GO WITH THE FLOW. WHATEVER."

— BIJOU HERD

IZZY & SOPHIA

What are your likes and dislikes?

Izze: I like TENNIS BALLS!!!!!!, and all that they entail, like playing fetch in the yard, in the house, in the river, dropping them in anyone's lap, dropping them in the dishwasher, dropping them in the toilet, dropping them in the laundry basket, pretty much dropping them anywhere until someone throws them. Also, I like car rides, mealtime and cuddling at night. I don't like being left home, or baths.

Sophia: I love to run through fields of tall grass and just feel the wind in my floppy ears. I don't like to be left at home.

What are your favorite activities?

IZZE: Ummm, did I mention tennis balls???

What do you do when you are home alone?

IZZE: I like to take naps in the laundry room 'cuz I have a really toasty fur coat and the tile floor in the laundry room keeps me nice and cool...and it's also right next to the garage so I can hear when Mom comes home and make sure I greet her at the door....with a tennis ball in my mouth.

SOPHIA: I have the best lookout spot ever. I sit on the back of the sofa and look out the floor-to-ceiling windows so I can keep an eye on every critter and bird in the yard.

Are you a morning or afternoon pet?

IZZE: I have a lot of energy, so I can pretty much be ready for an outing all day long. I do like to settle down at night and cuddle in the chair with Mom.

SOPHIA: I am like the Energizer bunny - I just go, go, go! Sometimes, Mom calls me her little "Meth Mutt." I'm not really sure what that is, but she just laughs when she says it, so it must just mean I'm really cute.

"SO MANY CRITTERS.....
SO LITTLE TIME!"
— SOPHIA GARTH

"LIFE'S SHORT.....
AND THERE ARE
SO MANY TENNIS
BALLS TO FETCH!"
—IZZE GARTH

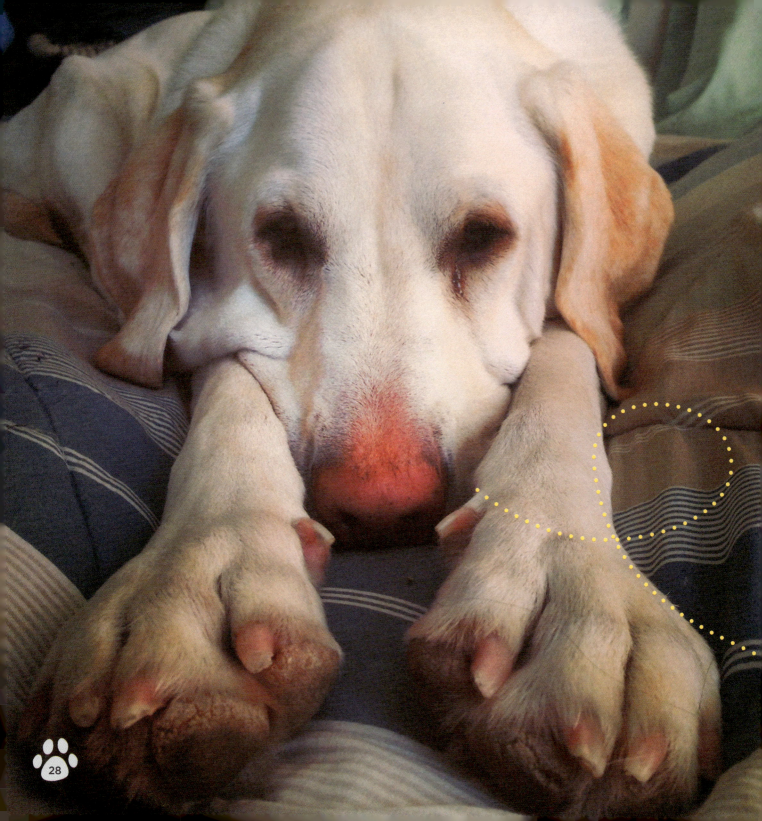

CLYDE

What are your likes and dislikes?

I like breakfast and dinner a lot. I do a smack lippin' dance for them. I dislike thunder storms and when I'm away from my mom.

What is your favorite treat?

Yummy Chummy's from Alaska. Paws and Claws has them and I love them!!

What is your favorite memory?

The day my best friend decided to adopt me. I was so confused and lost, but when she took me home I finally knew what love was and we've been on so many adventures together and both sleep well at night knowing we will wake up with each other. And I get breakfast.

Is there a specific story you would like to share?

When I was with my old owner he didn't do much with me so my sister and I use to wander the neighborhood and knock over trash and knock on doors for food. I gained a lot of weight. When I was taken away to the shelter they named us Bonnie and Clyde because we were so bad. But now I'm very good and have lost 100 pounds!

IS THERE REALLY A NEED FOR THIS ... TORTURE

"AS LONG AS I'M WITH MY BEST FRIEND, LIFE IS PERFECT."
— CLYDE SCROBLE

MILO & MILENA

MILENA SHARED HER THOUGHTS AND PASSED OVER THE RAINBOW BRIDGE IN 2015 DURING THE PRODUCTION OF THIS BOOK.

What do you do when you are home alone?

MILO: Oh gosh. Some days are better than others. One time, when I was a puppy, they let me out of that cage thing and I found that I have a taste for chewing up paper. I took my mom's cookbook, 'cause it has some nice residual smells, and shredded it. Then I took my dad's sketchbook and went to town on it. The house looked like play land with paper everywhere. My sister just hid in the corner. I tried to blame it on her, but it didn't work.

I like attacking my sister to just play with me as soon as my mom leaves – and then when she doesn't, that blue sponge thingy that's left out on the counter, I really like that its moist and full of flavor and rips up into nice tiny pieces. Ooo ooo...and I like corks too if she forgets to put them away.

MILENA: I have this regimen whereby I like to pick out certain shoes and put them all over the living room, then I find some garments to accessorize with them...then I still have problems with the couch or the bed or the bed or the couch thing.

> "SLEEP, PLAY SLEEP, EAT."
> – MILENA RENCH

Do you like your sibling?

MILO: I have one sister. Her name is Milena. She is kind of lame. She always gets the good bed. She has to be helped up the stairs and I can just run by her. She has lots of pills that she takes in her food while I have to wait drooling for mine. She does give me baths, which I really like and, shhhhh, she does provide some nice flavored poop sometimes, but my mom gets so angry with me.

MILENA: I don't like my little brother. He is a pain in the ass. He always wants to play and never sits still. He pushes me over all the time and he gets all the attention.

What is your favorite treat?

MILO: BBBBBOOOONNNEEESSS! I eat them really really really fast. Oh, and my sister's poop, but shhhh, don't tell my mom...

MILENA: For my 14th birthday, my mom made me steamed salmon and Frosty Paws. Oh my goodness, it was delicious. It was hot so it was hard to eat fast and then the Frosty Paws were cold, and I was getting annoyed with the whole licking thing so I tried to eat the whole container.

MILO: Oh yay yay yay! I forgot about that day! It was AWESOME!

"IT'S ALL FUN
AND GAMES
UNTIL SOMEONE
ENDS UP
IN A CONE."

– MIKITA RENCH
(MILO'S NEW BROTHER)

ECKO

THIS IS NOT LOOKING GOOD

What are your likes and dislikes?

I am a fan of Commando-belly rubs. They feel good in the summer grass or on the chilly snow. I also love hiking with Mom. Some of my favorite hikes include Sarvis Creek and the Devil's Causeway Loop – I love Colorado. I also love to chase rodents: One of my naughty habits is gulping down fuzzy rodents if they cross my path. I'm not sure what they taste like, it happens so fast, unless my Mom intervenes. I don't like sunscreen. Yuk. One of the disadvantages to being a red-headed Aussie is my nose gets sun burned, so Mom tries to keep me coated with sunscreen and "butt-butter" (the thick white stuff). But it IS yummy to lick off...

Do you like your housemates?

The reality is that I am the "Queen" of the land. My felines don't count (17-year-old Sid and 3-year-old Gucci).

What are your favorite activities?

Chilling with my family, especially when the kiddos are home. I also love to keep watch over the homestead, "Yampa Fleur de Lis"; I have black angus, fox and coyotes to manage.

"I DUB THEE...
MY BEST FRIEND
FOREVER"
— ANONYMOUS

P.S. ESPECIALLY IF YOU THROW THE BALL AND LET ME SWIM

TAFFY, ASTIN & TORY

What are your likes and dislikes?

TAFFY: I like to have my butt scratched and I like any food, all the time. I dislike when Mom tries to put me on a diet or when I'm being petted and my snooty sister barges right in like she's the queen of the family (yeah, right). I sort of like my cousin, Tory. She can be cute, but also annoying. I looooove water, I'm a great swimmer. And I like to lick people...a lot. I also really like to herd the cars when Mom takes us places. I really feel like I'm making a difference! And I don't like baths. But I like eating poop...sorry Mom and Dad.

ASTIN: I really like playing ball, going for hikes and riding in the car with Mom. I am also good at hanging out at home with my family. I like it when everyone is home. I don't like being in trouble or wearing one of my three naughty collars – one for barking, one so I don't go in my neighbor's yard, and I can't remember what the other one does. They are all scary and it is embarrassing to wear them. They make me sad. I also really don't like it when Mom and Dad pet Tory (more about her later), my annoying little sister who lives with us now.

TORY: I like playing and wrestling with other dogs, especially my big sister, Astin. I love Astin. I don't like it when people mess with me when I am trying to sleep. That is annoying.

I HATE WHEN I HAVE TO WEAR THIS DUMB THING

Do you like your siblings?

TAFFY: Define like. Astin likes to think she's the ruler of the house and I just have to put her in her place. Like, nu-uh, girlfriend. But, I will admit that I do like the company and I know she means well...most of the time.

ASTIN: Well, I love Taffy. She is bossy, but she has taught me a lot. She moves slower now because she is 14, but I love her. She is the boss of me. Tory...well, I like her, but she can be a pest – she always wants to wrestle and sometimes I just want to chill. Plus, because we are both the "little girls," sometime we both get in get trouble even when I didn't do anything. I liked being the baby of the family; now I'm the middle child. Remember the Brady Brunch? Just call me Jan.

TORY: Well, I live with my two older sisters, Taffy and Astin (they are technically my cousins, but we are close as sisters). I like having them to play with and hang out with. I think Astin pouts because she doesn't like it when her mom and dad pet me or I come in bed for snuggle time. Taffy can be a little crabby when I try to take her toys, but I love them very much.

What annoys you the most?

TAFFY: When Mom tries to put me on a diet. What does "tubular" mean anyways?? I think I look great. #bikiniseason.

What is your favorite treat?

TAFFY: GOLDFISH GOLDFISH GOLDFISH #PepperidgeFarmgoldfishrule

ASTIN: Frozen bones with peanut butter. Also Meanie Greenies and carrots. Not mixed together.

TORY: Treats hurt my tummy, but over the summer I have gotten to eat frozen peanut butter bones with Taffy and Astin – those are really yummy!

"SNUGGLING WITH YOUR FAMILY IN BED AT NIGHT IS THE BEST WAY TO END YOUR DAY."
— ASTIN SIEGEL

"EAT. SLEEP. EAT. LICK. EAT. REPEAT. EAT."
—TAFFY SIEGEL

Photo by Austin Colbert

41

"SHE WHO HIDES
THE MOST TOYS AND
SMASHES THE MOST
BUGS, WINS."
— TORY SIEGEL

43

DARWIN & NEWTON

> "A LONG LIFE RAMBLING IN THE WOODS IS THE MOST HEAVENLY DOG WAY TO LIVE." —DARWIN LAY

LOOK WHAT I CAN DO

Tell the readers a little about yourselves.

I'M NEWTON. I am a really orange Golden Retriever. I am 6 years old and was born right before Thanksgiving. Mom and Dad met me and my 11 brothers and sisters a few days later, in a little house in Oak Creek. I was out of that dog mayhem by Christmas Eve, snuggled on the couch like the spoiled little Christmas nugget I was meant to be. Within days, I mastered harassment of my big bro, Darwin.

I'M DARWIN. I'm 16 and I could care less what you think about me. That's why I'm so cool. Also, I'm an exceptionally handsome Golden, Lab, St. Bernard mutt. I keep close tabs on my humans and my pesky little brother, Newton, but I pretty much want everyone to leave me alone – unless you've got a hot dog, a long walk or a butt scratch to offer. I'm in to playing deaf these days, although I never fail to hear the farm-animal calls that announce the opening of the "cookie barn."

What are your likes and dislikes?

NEWTON: I like humans, long hikes, swimming, relocating giant stick piles out of the bonfire pit, forest romps, car rides...and snuggling with humans. I love my stuffed cow, which sometimes springs a leak, but Dad always sews him up so he looks like Frankencow. And he still moos, thank God. I do not like being left at home. Please take me with you. If you don't, I'm going to sprawl all over your bed and leave my orange fur everywhere, plus a whole bunch of really prickly burrs for extra punishment.

DARWIN: Mostly, I like to wander. I don't go as far afield as I used too. Back in the day, I was notorious for my epic backcountry treks. I always came home, but I was much maligned for the porcupine quills I regularly brought with me. I'm pretty proud that I schooled Mom and Dad on this for years. They are quill removal professionals. The only time they failed was the night before their wedding, when one of those darn pokers pierced my entire leg and it had to be surgically removed. Mom was mad because I had an ugly shaved leg as the ring bearer.

What is your favorite season and why?

NEWTON: I like summer, when the doors are open, so I can just go in and out and in and out and in and out all day long and no one gets mad at me when I change my mind half way in or out for the ten-thousandth time.

What is your favorite pastime?

DARWIN: If I'm not wandering, I mostly just lie around and save my energy for the next meander. Now that I'm getting old, I have suckered Mom and Dad into delivering meals directly to my pillow. That conserves energy for extra neighborhood monitoring trips: There are bones to be found. Thanks to hunters and the BLM land in my back yard, I have amassed the skeleton of at least an entire elk in my front yard over the years – you can't believe what tenacity it takes to drag an elk pelvis all the way home.

Is there anything else you would like to share with your readers?

DARWIN: I just have to say that I love kitties and I'm mad that I never got one of my own.

45

"PETTING, SCRATCHING, AND CUDDLING A DOG COULD BE AS SOOTHING TO THE MIND AND HEART AS DEEP MEDITATION AND ALMOST AS GOOD FOR THE SOUL AS PRAYER."

— DEAN KOONTZ, *False Memory*

LLOYD

What is your favorite activity?

Well, hiking and...rolling in bear poop. Or moose poop. I also enjoy elk and deer poop. And, if you can keep quiet, I'll let you in on a little secret; I occasionally indulge myself in a little poo treat every now and then. Shameful? A little. Embarrassing? Probably. But it is a tasty treat.

What is your most embarrassing moment?

Oh, do I have a tale of caution for any of you dogs out there that just happen to be able to read. There was a time where I, as many of my brethren do, would enjoy a quick dishwasher snack. Who doesn't love to get a little peanut butter off a dirty plate? (Don't worry, I never lick after eating animal poop.) One day, as I was doing a little after-dinner cleanup my collar got stuck. Instead of calmly waiting for help, I decided I would go into "crazy Lloyd" mode. I started jumping around uncontrollably, and, luckily I was able to pull myself from the dishwasher. Unfortunately the rack came with me and I couldn't shake it. In what was only a few seconds (but seemed like ages), my owner was able to free me from the rack. I calmed down, and everything seemed okay. That is, until I looked at the walls and the floor and there were stains all over. What I'm trying to say is, I pooped in my pants. But I don't wear pants. Alright, no more poop. I'm a mature, 8-year-old dog; I don't need to talk about poop all the time.

> "IF YOU AIN'T HIKING, YOU'RE SLEEPING."
> —LLYOD PREISSING

JOHNNY CASH

Tell the readers about your name.

My name is Johnny Cash (you know, like the famous singer), but we already have a Johnny in our family, so they call me Cash.

What are your likes and dislikes?

I love my two boys (Johnny and Braden), Bella (sibling) and Wall-E, the cat. My perfect moment is snuggling my two boys and Bella in front of the fire after a long day of playing with Rufus, a 150-pound Bloodhound puppy. I dislike cows and broccoli.

Do you like your siblings?

I love having a sibling. Bella has lovely and very tasty ears. Wall-E keeps me on my toes, as sometimes he gives me kitty hugs and then bites me. He's kind of confusing, but in the winter I get him back by smushing him into snowbanks.

What is your favorite memory?

When my mom picked me up and brought me home to my two little boys who like to have as much fun as I do.

JOSIE & JAKE

♡ xoxo ♡

Tell the readers how you two are related.

JOSEPHINE: My name is Princess Josephine Rundell, Josie for short. I was born April 9, 2007 in Denver and moved to Steamboat eight weeks later. I am a proud American Cocker Spaniel.

JACOB: My name is Jacob Rundell, and I am the son of Josie. Everyone calls me Jake for short. I was born May 26, 2009. I was the third of her pups, and I was actually born in the car on the way to the vet hospital!

What are your likes and dislikes?

JOSIE: I love to eat – especially ice cream! I love to ride in the car on Dad's lap and help him drive. Oh, and I also love to chase birds and eat horse "apples," which is perfect because we live on a ranch with horses. I DO NOT LIKE putting on my collar OR taking baths.

What do you do when you are home alone?

JAKE: When I am left home alone I howl and howl. Pathetic, really.

Do you like your housemates?

JOSIE: We have two horses, Mr. Buttons the cat, and Jake. I love having horses because they are always dropping treats for me in the fields. Mr. Buttons is okay for an old cat and Jake, well, I need to remind you that I am a Princess and he is just not in the same realm as me.

Is there anything else you would like to share?

JAKE: I would like to share my real story, my purpose. When I was four months old, my human Mom lost her only child, her son, in a car accident. For months she carried me around for comfort. I sat by her side and I licked the tears from her face. I have learned how to put her needs ahead of mine and to be there in full support. I have learned how to really listen, to hear and to see. I have become so connected to her that I know when I am really needed even if I am at the other end of the house. I even hear the silent cries. When I feel her pain I never leave her side. I follow her from room to room, sit close to her when she sits, and lay close to her at night. I hold her and soak up her pain and tears. I have learned the power of love and I know it has been that love that has helped her survive some really tough times. I am often referred to as her lifeline. I have found that the more love I give, the more love I have in me to give. I mentioned I love to be picked up and held, but I also know she loves picking me up and holding me. I believe that this mutual holding is the purest of love. Maybe that is what it is all about. Just being picked up and held.

xoxo

51

"I BELIEVE I WAS PUT ON THIS EARTH TO LOVE AND GIVE KISSES. THAT IS WHY I AM A HEELING FRIENDS DOG. I GIVE LOTS OF KISSES TO THE CHILDREN IN THE SCHOOL WHERE I GO AND READ. I AM VERY FRIENDLY TO EVERYONE I MEET AND I BELIEVE THAT IS HOW I AM SUPPOSED TO BE."

 —JOSIE RUNDELL

"I HAVE SO MUCH LOVE IN ME THAT SOMETIMES IT JUST WIGGLES OUT. I SEEM TO KNOW WHEN SOMEONE IS HURTING AND NEEDS A LITTLE EXTRA CARE. IT SOMETIMES TAKES ME A WHILE TO WARM UP TO SOMEONE, BUT ONCE I DO I AM EXTREMELY CONNECTED AND LOVING."

 —JAKE RUNDELL

ALMA ROSE

What are your likes and dislikes?

I like walking, running, jumping, sniffing, eating, treats, people, some kids, people food, car rides with my face out the window...pretty much my likes would be life. I dislike dogs I don't like, baths and people touching my toes.

What do you do when you are home alone?

Guard the house and sleep. If I am displeased with the amount of time I have been left alone, or with the amount of time I think I'm going to be left alone, I go upstairs to my mom's bathroom garbage and take each piece of trash out and spread the pieces on the floor so she will be aware of my displeasure.

What is your favorite memory?

Living in the wilderness for a month. There were no leashes, no rules, no roads, no people, just squirrels and trees and snow and I could go wherever I wanted. However, the sleeping accommodations were a little under par for what I'm used to. The tent was a little small for my liking and the bed not as cushiony as I prefer. But overall, I'd take living in the wild over this whole house thing any day.

"WHATEVER YOU CHOOSE TO DO, DO IT WITH YOUR WHOLE HEART."
—ALMA ROSE MCKINLEY

HENRY

What do you do when you are home alone?

Claw the furniture.

What is your favorite memory?

Mom and Dad saw my ad in the Steamboat Today. I was a stray that was found and turned in on Seedhouse Road; the staff at the shelter named me Henry. As it turned out, Henry was the name of my dad's grandfather as well as the name of my mom's mother's adopted cat. It was serendipity. When Dad came back into the cat room at the shelter for the second time, I knew I had a home!

"HAPPINESS IS FINDING THE PERFECT SUNNY SPOT, WHICH I DO DAILY BECAUSE I FOLLOW THE SUN ALL THROUGH THE HOUSE."

— HENRY KIRKPATRICK

KENAI

What are your likes and dislikes?

I love to be outside during any season. I love my sister, Addie (a Golden Retriever), who is like a mother to me. I also really love leftover elk steaks, watermelon and hugs from Mom. I do not like conflict and am very sensitive to angry energy.

What annoys you the most?

I get annoyed when I have to be on a leash; that's why I like hiking in the wilderness away from the crowds.

What is your favorite memory?

My favorite memory was the day my family adopted me. I was born a sheep dog, but I was thrown off the back of my master's truck and he didn't stop for me. A nice person picked me up and took me to the vet. I had shattered my femur. My old master did not come for me. Each day, a woman would sit with me and pet me until one day she adopted me and took me home. My new family had dogs, cats, horses and more. Everyone loved me and helped me wag my tail more often to get through all the pain. The day I went home with my new mom is my best memory.

KONA

> "THE SHADIER THE DECK, THE LONGER THE NAP."
> — KONA ARMSTRONG

What are you likes and dislikes?

I like tummy rubs, giving kisses, rolling in snow or dust, and chilling like a villain on the deck enjoying the heat in the summer. My dislikes include when people try to take piggy back rids on me, dress me up, and cats, squirrels, and YAPPY DOGS.

Do you like your housemate?

No, I do not like my housemate, "Oreo," because she squeaks very loud and shares carrots with Skeet (my owner's son). FYI, Oreo is a Guinea Pig. Worthless, in my opinion.

What is your favorite activity?

Hanging with my family.

" WHEN YOU NEED A FRIEND YOU NEED A DOG CAT OR ANY PET OF ANY SPECIES. PETS ARE THE MOST LOYAL FRIEND YOU CAN HAVE SO CURL ON UP TO YOUR BEST FURRY FRIENDS WHEN YOU READ THIS."

— J GIRL

FRODO BAGGINS & LUNA

Ever heard of the infamous Honey Badger? The Honey Badger has thrilled, disgusted and amused many an Internet surfer looking for ways to avoid work: "Honey Badger don't care!"

Mom and Dad are so fortunate to have their own live-action version: "Honey-Jacks," the ferocious Jack Russell Terrier cousin to the Honey Badger. We are Frodo Baggins Lorenz and Luna Lovegood Lorenz and together we thrill, disgust and amuse visitors to our backyard wilderness with our adventures and hunting antics. Do you find dead, half chewed, dis-engorged rodents disgusting? We don't care – the more disgusting the better!

We are normally adorable, loving, obedient and easy going little dogs. Even outdoors on the ranch, we are eager and helpful companions while doing chores, going on horseback rides or going on any outing. That is, until we hear the "chirp" of a chipmunk or detect the whiff of mouse. Then suddenly, with a flurry of dust, we are off in a blur! We stop at nothing, and nothing can stop us when a rodent is detected.

One day, Mom and Dad were moving a stack of lumber sheets from a pallet into the barn. Both of us were in an excited state...we could smell the mice under the stack. With quivering tails, and screeching yips, we scurried from one side to the other until the moment....UP came the last sheet! Underneath was our stuff of dreams; three mouse nests, each with an entire litter of mice! Thirty to 40 mice scattered like dropping a bowl of marbles on the floor. Quick as that we flew into action!

Snatch! Chomp! Swallow!
Snatch! Chomp! Swallow!
Snatch! Chomp! Swallow!

As fast as the mice could scatter, we could swallow.

Now, our bellies can only hold so many mice; but did we quit when full? Never! We never gave up our battle. Instead it became Snatch! Chomp! FLING! Snatch! Chomp! FLING! Snatch! Chomp! FLING! What a sight! Mice, one after the other, flying through the air until all the mice were gone.

When the carnage was over, and after the swollen bellies receded, it became apparent that we did not come through unscathed. We suffered through many days of upset stomachs, nasty mouse gas (which we thought smelled fabulous), and scratchy throats from the mice we'd swallowed whole.

We recovered completely, and are again ready at a moment's notice to fly into battle in our tenacious quest to rid the world of rodents. At least the ones in our Honey-Jack world.

HARLEY DAVIDSON, CHARLIE, DENALI & ISIS

What are your likes and dislikes?

HARLEY: I like my mum. I really like to follow her everywhere she goes, bathroom, closet, laundry, doesn't matter and space is irrelevant as I can squeeze anywhere. I like to shake my head and see where and on whom I can hit my slobber (I have watched Sister Mickinley change several times before school). I also like to stomp and chase the cat, Isis; sometimes I scare her so much she hisses and stands on two legs. It's pretty hilarious. I don't like going to the pet ranch/kennel. I see my mum get all teary eyed and it makes me sad. It's loud and I don't sleep or eat. It doesn't happen often though.

ISIS: I really like darting as fast as I can up and down the beams and scaring the family. I am also greatly humored by my move of "stop, drop and roll" right as a human walks past; sometimes they laugh and play with me, other times, when they are not paying attention, they also step on me!

CHARLIE: I like my dragon toy.

What annoys you the most?

CHARLIE: Young boys who tease and try to intimidate me – they are the reason I left my first home and I am still mad about it. (Even though I much prefer my forever family now).

DENALI: I am annoyed by how EVERYONE makes such a fuss of my brothers and sometimes forgets about me. They are cute and all, but seriously, they are massive and can sometimes just have no clue at all.

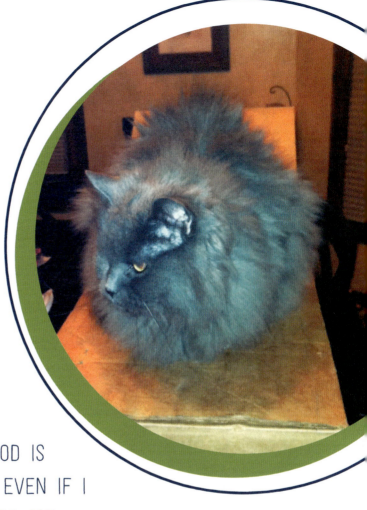

"GET OUT THERE AND ENJOY IT. YOU DON'T KNOW WHAT TOMORROW WILL BRING."

–HARLEY MCATEE

"KEEP TRYING, ESPECIALLY WHERE FOOD IS CONCERNED. I WILL TRY EVERYTHING, EVEN IF I DON'T LIKE IT OR IF IT ISN'T GOOD FOR ME. I WILL TRY IT AND TRY IT AGAIN, AGAIN AND AGAIN AND AGAIN!"

– DENALI MCATEE

"OUTSMART THE HUMANS. IT IS NOT HARD. THEY ARE PUTTY IN MY HAND!" – ISIS MCATEE

HONEY BADGER

What do you do when you are home alone?

When Mom and Dad are gone I'm tied up or locked on the porch because I tend to wander off to find one of my friends in the neighborhood to play with. We don't cause any trouble, but the dog catcher thinks otherwise. Sometimes, when I'm tied up I get bored and dig holes. When I'm not digging holes, I sleep.

Do you like your housemates?

There are three other dogs and two cats in our family. I like the other dogs, but they are getting kind of old and don't like to play as much as I do. I try to get them to play, but sometimes they get cranky and just snarl at me. The cats don't have too much to do with me and they just try to stay out of my way. I'm half afraid of the one cat; she is mean.

What is your favorite treat?

My favorite treat is the one I'm eating at the time. If I had to pick just one I'd have to say freshly caught mice and voles.

Is there anything else you would like to share with your readers?

O.K., I'll tell this one more time and that's it. When I was a puppy, and before my people had to install an expensive hidden electric fence (that they have since found out is useless), I used to go into my neighbor's house through a little door meant just for dogs. I knew how these worked because we have a couple of them too. Well anyhow, inside were bowls full of dog food. I guess they had too much food because there was still some left over. That never happens at my house. So I ate it. I also found the storage bins where these nice folks kept their dog food. It was a little bit of work, but I managed to pull them off the shelf and untie the straps around them so I could get inside and eat that food too. After all that food I was tired so I went into the bedroom of the humans that belong to my friends, I licked the toes sticking out from under the covers and jumped in bed with them. I found out later that was not such a good idea.

" PLAY HARD, SLEEP
OFTEN AND EAT
WHENEVER I CAN."
— HONEY BADGER ECHTERMEYER

POUDRE *"the wonder dog"*
MCCAULLEY

Can you tell us a little bit about your background?

I was in the shelter for a while after being found wandering around. I was just a baby then, so I don't really remember why I was wandering around, but I was scared and lonely. Then someone, who seemed real nice, picked me up and put me in a cage in a truck, and then in another cage at the shelter. The weather was very cold, and I was cold. There were some awesome volunteers there who took me out and played with me, especially some nice kids. I was sick then. Nobody realized how fun I could be, because I just didn't feel well. Little did they know. Maggie from the Routt County Humane Society suggested that my family (those nice kids) foster me. Awesome idea because NO WAY could they take me back to the shelter! It was my beginning of a great life.

> "MY PLAY IS MY WORK."
> — POUDRE MCCAULLEY

What is your favorite activity/pastime?

WHAT DO I LIKE? DUH!!!! FRISBEE, FRISBEE, FRISBEE!

My family refers to it as the "F-word," but I totally know what they are talking about. They should KNOW that Border Collies can spell. I try and leave my Frisbee wherever I think they are going to be, which is sometimes hard to predict. That way I can leave my Frisbee so they will think about throwing it (sometimes they just need to be cued). I even try and leave it where they don't have to move to get it. Having my ancestors predict what the sheep would do really comes in handy. Sometimes I am so connected with them. And the "Border Collie stare!" That comes down through the generations, too. Frisbee, their eyes, Frisbee, their eyes, Frisbee, their eyes.

What is your favorite season and why?

That is a hard one. Trails with the horses, or trails in the snow. I have booties, coats and sunglasses, so sometimes when it is really cold, it takes them a long time to dress me, and I feel a bit silly around other dogs. When it gets cold, though, I've got it made and it makes it all worth while. So...I guess it would have to be summer, based on the clothing thing.

What is your favorite memory?

I think it might be the time that I won an agility competition and beat all the dogs even when I had not trained for that event. It was a bit of an insult when someone said "Not bad for a rescue," but my mom and I were both saying "Woo Hoo!" It made me very proud that I could focus and be a partner.

I AM Wonder Dog

RENNY

"LIFE IS GREAT!"

– RENNY MEGLEN

Can you tell us a little bit about yourself?

My name is Renny and I was born December 20, 2004. Life was good enjoying Mom and Dad as an only dog, but then they decided I should have puppies. Wow, that was yucky! I had puppies together with my prior housemate, KC, on July 20, 2009. I had eight puppies and thought that was the end of that.

Do you like your housemates?

Well, almost four years after I had the eight puppies, one of my puppies, Mango, had a litter (better her than me) and she had 11 puppies. WOW, that was more yucky! Mom and Dad decided that they should keep one, so now I live with my grandpuppy, Whitney, who was born on April 30, 2013. I tolerate her okay, but she is always trying to take the attention away from me so I have to compete for attention from Mom and Dad. We compete for the tennis ball too.

What is your favorite treat?

One of our favorite treats is iceberg lettuce. I like the crunch and we get lots of it.

What annoys you the most?

I like my meals more regularly – like when I first wake up, and then at about 5 p.m. I start bothering Mom and Dad trying to tell them that it's time to eat. They aren't tuned into my schedule.

TAFFY

Taffy Emerson shared her thoughts and passed over the Rainbow Bridge in 2015

Can you tell us a little bit about yourself?

My name is Taffy. I'm a 13-year-old Standard Poodle who was adopted by Mom and Dad from Poodle Rescue in Phoenix. Until I was 10 months old, I was kept in a crate all day long because my owners worked all day. Then the lady who lived next door convinced them that this was no life for a dog, and they gave me up. Whew!

What is your favorite memory?

My favorite memory is going llama trekking in the Flat Tops with Mom and Dad. I knew I had to stay away from the llamas, but as long as I kept an eye on where they and my people were, I could roam and find new smells to investigate. I didn't really like carrying my own panniers with my water, a bowl and some lunch, but since everyone else carried a pack, I had to as well.

"LIFE IS GOOD"

— GIPPER ROACH

Photo by Austin Colbert

TUCKER & GIPPER

I HATE WHEN GIPPER BARKS. I HOPE THEY PUT THIS ON HIM

What are your likes and dislikes?

Tucker: I am sort of obsessed with tennis balls. I love to roll on them in the yard when my mom and dad won't throw them. I like to try to drink coffee. I love my mom and dad's bed, I love, love, love swimming, and my new favorite is chasing Mr. Fox with Gipper. OMG, I almost forgot...my favorite thing of all is to try to catch all the snow in my mouth when someone shovels. I do NOT like sitting in the way back of the car or when my family leaves me home.

Gipper: I love to be snuggled, rubbed and loved on at all times. I love sleeping right on people's feet and I love begging for food. I love to bark and I love to play ball. I love my brother, Tucker, and I love getting the better bed before him and lying on my back and dozing off with my legs in the air. I LOVE, LOVE sticking my head underwater and getting rocks. I hate being left home alone without my brother, and when no one will throw the ball for me.

What do you do when you are home alone?

Tucker: I cry and howl and look out the window yearning for anyone to come home and play. I usually gather shoes and chase my tail in circles.

Gipper: I watch Tucker.

What annoys you the most?

TUCKER: When my parents pack bags to go on vacation and when they put my tennis balls up high so I can't reach them.

GIPPER: When I get put in time-out for barking at the ball.

What is your favorite treat?

TUCKER: Bacon

GIPPER: More Bacon than Tucker.

BUDDY

"MY PHILOSOPHY IS TO EAT, EXERCISE, AND ENJOY MY GREAT STEAMBOAT LIFE!"
—BUDDY ARAGON

DO THEY REALLY NEED TO MEASURE MY FOOD?

What is your favorite activity?

I love running up Emerald with Granddad. Also, I used to love surfing behind our boat with Jeff, my dad who now lives in Texas. But, one time I tried to jump from the surfboat back into the boat. I missed and was barely hanging onto the back of the boat and then fell back into the water. So now I am not so into surfing.

Do you like being an only pet?

I love being the top dog. My grandparents' other granddogs come to visit and I can't wait until they go home.

What is your favorite season and why?

I love winter. Grandma takes me for walks around our property. I love bounding through the deep snow. It makes me feel like a deer. However, I also love summer when Grandpa takes me on the paddleboard down the Yampa River!

What annoys you the most?

When my dog dish is empty. I used to bang on my dog dish and either Grandma or Grandpa would feed me. Then, I started gaining weight – now they measure my food. Dang!

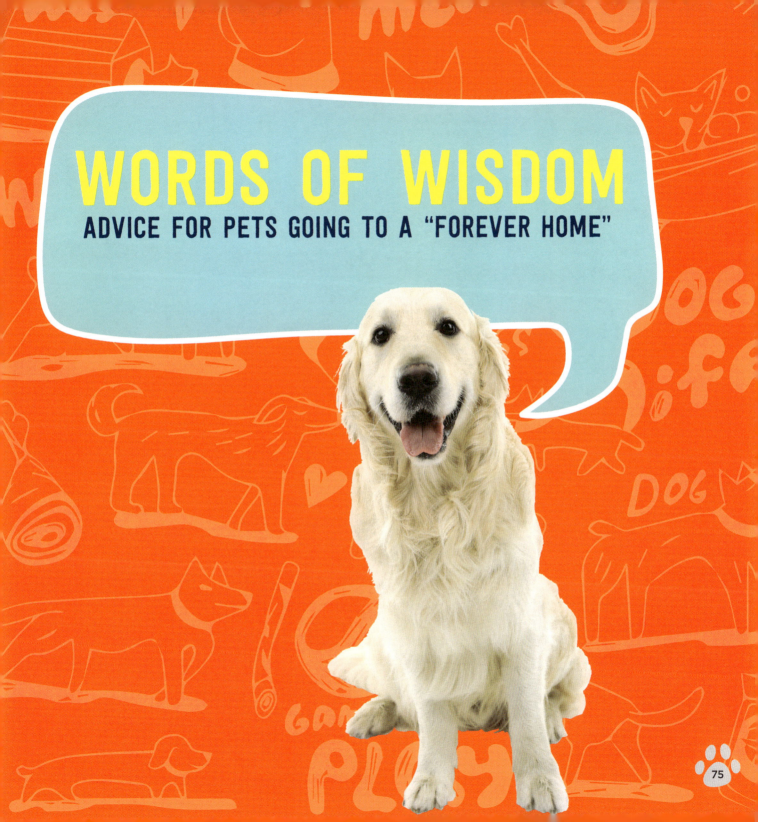

WORDS OF WISDOM

ADVICE FOR PETS GOING TO A "FOREVER HOME"

Cabot Weaver: Make sure you make yourself available for tummy rubs.

Pico Weaver: Be friendly and easy-going.

Flavias Borden

Try not to chew on part of the house or anything else that can't be thrown away.

CLYDE SCROBLE

Hang in there; it only gets better from here on out.

LEROY & FRED ZOLTANI

Leroy: Accidents happen, but don't pee in the bed!

Fred: Its ok to neck snuggle.

Bijou & Felix Herd

Bijou: Well, I was lucky. I was kicked out of my home and dropped at a shelter and suddenly found myself with a rescue lady who eventually talked Dad into keeping me. I was the newest pet in a rather odd bunch – three other dogs and a cat, all with their own turf. Mom and Dad kept me because I got along with everybody and was willing to play with the "crazy young dog" who needed a playmate. I guess that's my advice – get along with everybody. Okay, the cat was a bit of a challenge. I did chase him for a while, just for the kicks of it. I didn't intend to hurt him. But I did eventually quit and they decided to keep me.

Feliz: My advice is to be incredibly cute and bubbly. It worked for me. I had chronic health issues as a puppy, which is why I got dumped at a vet's office and taken to a shelter. Mom and Dad rescued me and nursed me back to health. They kept me, even though they knew I'd be expensive my entire life. I'm irresistibly cute. I wiggle my butt. I cuddle. They didn't even consider giving me up.

COOPER MATTOX

Try to listen and do your best to follow the rules. But most importantly, make sure your family knows how much you love them. Be loyal. Be a good listener. Always show them how happy you are to see them.

Sophia & Izze Garth

Izze: Love your families unconditionally and be oh so grateful to have loving forever homes.

Sophia: Just be so so grateful that you have a forever home...cuz I know what it's like to have only part-time homes.

KENAI BYE

Trust that you are already loved, and wag a lot.

BUDDY LAMB

Christen every room with a spritz of urine; make sure the others know it's yours.

HENRY KIRKPATRICK

Don't stress over your new surroundings. Take your time to feel comfortable in your new home.

Milo & Milena Wrench

Milo: Don't listen, always give a cute innocent face, and hopefully you'll get some treats.

Milena: Don't allow your family to get a little brother!

NEWTON LAY

Dog friends, my advice is to be a big lover and play up your really adorable pleading eyes. Also, try to have good manners. This is how you get everything you want and more. But don't ever roll in horse poop: Mom and Dad get really mad.

CASH DUTY

Don't potty in the house. It isn't polite and makes Mom mad.

POUDRE McCAULLEY

Do your best. I mean, really. Don't chew up their stuff. Usually they will be back, so don't panic. Just be patient. You will be rewarded, and so will they.

Honey Badger Echtermeyer

Do as I say and not as I do. By that I mean don't chew things up (I chewed up lots of stuff), stay close to home (I tend to roam), don't dig holes (I like to dig), and only eat what you are given (I like to see what else is on the counter or stove top). In a nutshell, just be a dog and do what dogs do.

Charlie D'Ambrosio

Just keep loving. That is all that matters.

TESSA KOCIK

The first thing you should do when you get to your new home is lie down on your back, legs up and let your new family scratch away – it's the best! You are home now.

KONA ARMSTRONG
Respect your family and make sure they get plenty of kisses.

78

TAFFY, ASTIN & TORY SIEGEL

TAFFY: Listen closely amateurs... PUPPY DOG EYES. They fix every thing. Peed on the carpet? Puppy dog eyes. Ate your sister's food? Puppy dog eyes. Rolled in poop? PUPPY DOG EYES!

ASTIN: If you are going to your forever home in Routt County, Colorado you have hit the Puppy Jackpot! Love your family and follow the rules. Oh, and don't chew up their stuff. That usually doesn't work out well.

TORY: Don't chew up everything and especially stay away from electrical cords and shoes. Be friendly, give love and licks.

Cali Brander

All five of us furry kids are a lively bunch and bring much joy and laughter daily to this family. If any of you shelter animals are looking for that forever home, make sure you look real hard at the human's forehead. If it says "softy" across it, you've got a "paw-in" for being adopted. Just make sure you show your best side and you'll live happily ever after.

Mango & Melon Sweers

Mango: You are lucky to be loved so don't roll in horse poo every day.

Melon: Try not to jump on the kitchen island and eat the butter.

TUCKER & GIPPER ROACH

Sleep through the night, try not to poop or vomit in the house, and if you must, please don't do it on the carpet. Don't stand or lay on the floor in the kitchen, don't bark unless you really need to, and no unnecessary loud licking. Be good, be happy! Love life!

ROXY TRACY

Yay! Your people are there to love, care and teach you everything you need to know. Cherish every moment and always be grateful for your forever home.

LOLA MADER

Trust that your new family has your best interests in mind. They did pick YOU!

TAFFY EMERSON

Be a worthy pet. Learn what is expected of you. Show your love and your People will love you in return. A "forever home" is the best place in the world to be.

Tuesday & Yeti Barr

Tuesday: Start early and be consistent in training your new owner. Humans are not the brightest species, but with a little patience and work, you'll be eating out of their hands in no time, literally.

Yeti: If you hear the word "bath", run under the bed and wedge yourself along the back wall. Do not come out for treats no matter how tempting. Not even baked chicken.

PENNY PAINTER

If you want your new family to love you, let them know when you have to relieve yourself. Don't spaz out for food or walks, and DO NOT chew stuff!

ZEPHYR PARSONS (favorite quote)

"Never slow down, never look back, live each day with adolescent verve and spunk and curiosity and playfulness. If you think you're still a young pup, then maybe you are, no matter what the calendar says."
—by JOHN GROGAN

SAM SMITH

Love your mom and dad and they will love you right back.

EMMA

What are your likes and dislikes?

I like to sleep a lot (I'm getting older), especially in corners or under furniture where I feel secure. I like to sit outside on my back deck and look at the world. I also like to go on walks – with or without leash – but I can't handle the long hikes that I used to love so much due to arthritis in my legs.

I dislike having a bath and going in water above my knees – and I especially don't like getting my face wet. I really don't like fireworks or hot weather. I seek shade on my walks or in my yard if the sun is too strong.

What do you do when you are home alone?

Well, I always love to get into waste baskets in bedrooms and bathrooms. (I would go for the real trash with food and scraps, but that darn cabinet is too hard for me to open.) I love to shred tissues into tiny pieces and scatter them on the floor. Sometimes, I get mad when I am left at home and go to the basement and pee on the carpet in my little special spot – I always try to do it in the same place. The pee gets cleaned but my nose can smell it out. I know my folks get angry when I do this, so I don't do it too often, just enough to let them know I have feelings. After the folks have been gone a while, I like to sit at the front door and look out the little side window to see when they drive up. Oh, and if by chance when I am alone there happens to be some food or food wrappers anywhere in my reach – including in purses, suitcases, or on counter – I will enjoy gobbling it up!

Do you like being an only pet?

I am currently the only pet and I love it. I used to have a sister, Cocoa, who I was super close with. For the first six years of my life she was my constant companion. I followed her everywhere. She died about six years ago and for a long time I missed her very much.

THE BRANDER BUNCH

PACKER: My Mom and Dad named me Packer, as in the Green Bay Packers. I am a transplant from a small town in Wisconsin. I'm an 8-year-old male Golden Retriever. I was actually born on the day that Mom and Dad's first Golden was hit by a car, but I'd rather not say any more, as that still hurts Mom's and Dad's hearts.

MILLIE: I'm Packer's sister, and as Packer knows, I AM the Queen in this house. I was a adopted when I was 6 months old and came with a bit of baggage, but my parents adore me anyway.

CALI: I'm Cali, a.k.a. "Mama," THE QUEEN of the household, even if Millie claims she is. My mom fostered me six years ago, back in Wisconsin when I was a young mother who had just delivered four kittens at the shelter. I heard her tell Dad, that no, we wouldn't be keeping any of the animals they fostered. That had been "the deal" when she spoke to him about being a foster. So, I initiated my "win-them-over plan."

What is your favorite activity?

PACKER: My mom is a firm believer that a tired dog is a good dog, so we get at least an hour of off leash walking a day, besides hanging outside all day watching her talk to her flowers or watching her shovel Steamboat's monstrous snows.

MILLIE: My most favorite thing in the whole world to do is chase chippies (chipmunks). In Wisconsin, I had underground fencing so the chippies knew just how far I could run to chase them. They'd sit past the line and put their thumbs in their ears and wiggle them and squeak at me, "Nana, nana, nana!" Not here! I have the whole property to run.

What do you do when you are home alone?

MILLIE: If I think my parents have left me for too long and I'm bored with the other furry animals in this house, I root through any waste baskets I can get to and pull out the used Kleenex and tear it up. I don't earn a lot of points doing that.

What annoys you the most?

MILLIE: Neither Packer nor I "retrieve" balls unless my mom throws one for a visiting dog. Then we try and act like we like to do that dumb sport. The game is short lived. We don't like other dogs' slobber. In fact, if my mom is generous on a neighborhood walk and shares our water bottle with another dog, WE don't drink out of it. Cooties!

TUESDAY &
YETI

Yeti Barr shared her thoughts and passed over the Rainbow Bridge in 2015 during the production of this book

What are your likes and dislikes?

Tuesday: I like chasing the cat and anything else that moves, bossing Yeti around, swimming and children. I dislike baths, leashes and insubordinates (anyone stepping out of line).

Yeti: I like wallowing in the river (feeling weightless feels like heaven), sitting outside in blizzards and pouring rain, and baked chicken. I dislike sneaky cats, loud noises and strangers.

What are your favorite pastimes?

Yeti: Napping and playing the game "Which house did I steal this from?" (which entails my bringing home items from neighbors properties at night and watching my human friends try to figure out where it came from the next morning).

What do you do when you are home alone?

TUESDAY: Mix cocktails for Junco (the cat).

Do you like your housemate?

YETI: What housemate?

What is your favorite season and why?

YETI: Garbage Day Season

What annoys you the most?

TUESDAY: When Mom shuts the car door and I have to squeeze out the window to follow her into the store. Also, the word "no."

Are you a morning or afternoon pet?

YETI: Actually I prefer the night – cooler, less strangers, more cover to raid trash on garbage day.

"HERE ARE SOME OF MY FAVORITE LESSONS
I HAVE LEARNED SO FAR:

ESPECIALLY TO SHARE WITH MY NEW BROTHER STEVIE

1. NEVER PASS UP THE OPPORTUNITY TO GO FOR
A JOY RIDE.

2. ALLOW THE EXPERIENCE OF FRESH AIR AND THE
WIND IN YOUR FACE TO BE PURE ECSTASY.

3. WHEN LOVED ONES COME HOME, ALWAYS RUN
AND GREET THEM.

4. WHEN IT'S IN YOUR BEST INTEREST, ALWAYS
PRACTICE OBEDIENCE.

5. LET OTHERS KNOW WHEN THEY'VE INVADED
YOUR TERRITORY.

6. TAKE NAPS AND ALWAYS STRETCH BEFORE RISING.

7. RUN, ROMP AND PLAY DAILY.

8. EAT WITH GUSTO AND ENTHUSIASM."

— ROXY PIEKNIK

ROXY

What is your favorite activity?

Besides playing in the snow, chasing tennis balls, hiding in tall grass and then pouncing... my next favorite activity is running. I love cruising around at top speed, sometimes I like to jib around just for fun on patrol. Patrolling my farm is absolutely an important daily activity. Every day, I do a full loop (a bunch of times actually) and mark my spots, and look for predators (chipmunks, bunnies, grouse, mice or fox mostly). Normally, everything is under control; but sometimes I get excited and try to chase a bigger animal away (elk, deer or moose) – they are definitely invaders. My people won't let me out at night alone, otherwise I would tell those coyotes what's up for sure. I do anyways, from my porch, even if I am 10 feet off the ground...

What do you do when you are home alone?

I am not home alone too much. When I was little, I used to get to work with Dad everyday in the truck. I didn't like being home alone when I was little and would chew on things to keep myself busy. Sometimes I wasn't even home alone and I would enjoy a shoe treat for fun. My people didn't really like that too much. Nowadays on the farm, I spend my home alone time napping in the cool basement, on the deck under my umbrella, on my people's bed, the guest bed, sometimes the couch or even in the back of Momma's truck if it's home. I also like to rearrange the house and bring shoes, shirts, hats and socks outside on my bed or other various places about

the house. Couch corners, the bed and the back of Momma's truck are my favorite hiding spots. If I get a funny feeling about the weather, I like to bring everything inside. I even tried to bring my bed through my doggy door once; it didn't fit, but I made some alterations that I thought were pretty cool. If I can sneak it outside, burying in the yard is awesome! I once got Momma's shoe, a shirt, and Dad's socks and shoes tucked away in secret spots never to be found again. I am such a good hider of things!

What is your favorite memory?

I was found by the side of the road as a puppy and brought to Lifeline Puppy Rescue (a no-kill puppy shelter) in Longmont, Colorado, when I was 10 weeks old. I was very dirty from hiding in tall grass and hunting out on my own. I was so grateful to have Momma and Dad show up one day (while I was sleeping on my friend, the Boxer mix) and give me kisses and love and want to take me home with them. I gave them loads of kisses too and they seemed to like that. We took a big long car ride and I slept all the way on my new momma's lap. We even stopped and played in this funny white stuff on top of a mountain on the way there!

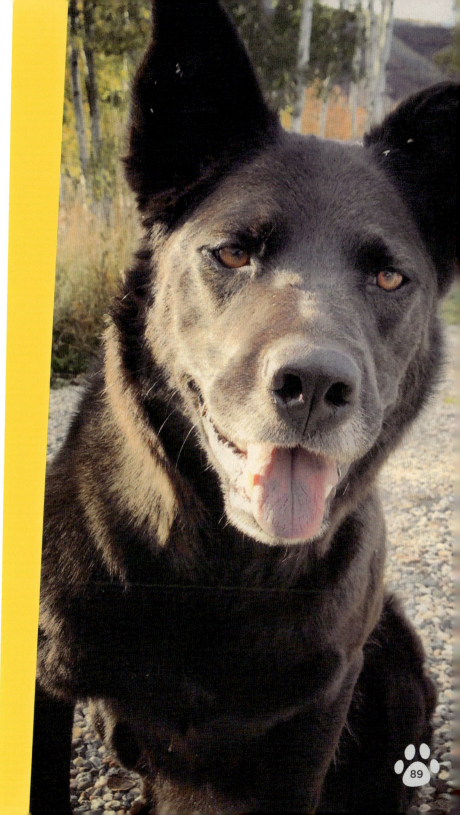

TESSA

What are your likes and dislikes?

I like kids, especially Olivia and Nick, dog treats, going to the lumberyard, playing with squirrels, lying by the fireplace, and riding in the car with my head out the window, no matter how cold it is. I dislike lightening, fireworks and being left behind.

What is your favorite memory?

Leaving the shelter and my very first powder day.

What is your favorite activity?

Running on the mountain trails (and off trail), diving in piles of deep powder and meeting other dogs.

SAM SMITH

A.K.A "OREO"

What is your favorite activity?

I really like to go on hikes with my mom and play rough house with my best friend, Tessa.

What are your likes and dislikes?

I love to dig in the dirt, hide things in the dirt and then find them later. I do NOT like swimming. Even puddles freak me out a little.

What is your favorite memory?

The day I met my family: Mom, Emmy and Paige. Those two girls make laugh with all their dancing and singing. Sometimes I even sing along with them.

Is there a specific story you want to share?

I was named after the singer Sam Smith. Every time one of his songs comes on the radio, Emmy and Paige hop up and down and sing to me. I sing right back and that makes them giggle.

YES I HID THE TOYS

ZOE

What are your likes and likes and dislikes?

LIKES:

- My mom and dad, of course!
- Vegetable and fruit scraps
- Laying in the water like a hippo
- When my mom and dad walk thru the door
- Napping is pretty great too
- SNOW!

DISLIKES:

- When other dogs try to fight with me
- When my mom gets anxious when we take walks together
- Grooming...of any sort, especially when they squirt that smelly stuff in my ears
- Heat
- When people touch my paws...I really hate that
- Lightening, thunder, fireworks

What is your favorite season and why?

Hummm...that's a tough one. I love summer because of camping, but winter...I LOVE the cold snow on my belly. And have you ever tasted fresh snow? Or stuck your face in it...it's the best. I love freshies!!

What annoys you the most?

Grooming. A bath isn't so bad but the combing after, I can't stand it. Oh! In the winter, when the snowballs get stuck in my paws...that's the worst.

What is your favorite pastime?

Camping! That usually means I don't have to be on a leash. I get to run around and sniff... EVERYTHING, EVERYWHERE! There is usually water involved and I'm part Hippo so that works out really well. After dinner, I get to lick the dinner plates...I love that. And I get to climb up on the bed in the morning and lie on top of Dad...and lick his face until he gets out of bed. Pretty much, there are no rules when we go camping.

"PAY ATTENTION TO ME WHEN I BARK, FEED ME VEGGIES AND ALL WILL BE RIGHT IN THE WORLD." –ZOE COOK

93

LOLA

What are your likes and dislikes?

I LOVE squirrels. They are so much fun to play with! I like climbing trees (when I can) to get closer to the squirrels. They throw things at me sometimes, but that's okay because they're so much fun to chase. I also love food – any food. My favorite treat is peanut butter in a Kong; it'll keep me distracted for hours on end. I also love people. I'm told I'm a very friendly dog; my whole body wiggles when I get to meet or hang out with people!

I hate nighttime because it is dark outside. I don't like not being able to see where noises are coming from. Once, there were elk in the backyard, and I could hear them but not see them. Now I'm scared to go potty at night, so I just bark really loud until they hear me. More than anything though, I hate fireworks! They really scare me.

What is your favorite activity/ pastime?

I love to run! Sometimes I just get this feeling that I need to run. It's weird because I could be sniffing a bush one minute and the next minute I'm sprinting around the yard! I don't really get tired from running; I could run for days. I'm told that I like to run and am good at running because I have Greyhound in me, so I like to show this off to the neighbor dogs. I like being a "45 mph couch potato." After running, all I want to do is lie down and cuddle!

What annoys you the most?

I get so annoyed when my mom sleeps in MY bed. She says it's hers, but I sleep in it more! I hate having to move so she can have some room. I like being able to have my space.

> "DON'T WALK THROUGH LIFE: RUN!"
> — LOLA MADER

PUPPY

Hello, My name is Puppy. Don't give me crap for the "unoriginal" name. When I was living in Switzerland, I actually had a really interesting name that seemed quite distinguished. For whatever reason, when I moved here to Steamboat, Balzac didn't cut it. Something about sounding like "ball sack" didn't sit well with my mom, Caroline. Don't get these people sometimes! Where's their culture?

What are your likes and dislikes?

I have a very evolved palette, which doesn't lend itself well to the lame treats people at the bank are always trying to give me. I try to feign interest, but the truth is, who would eat that crap? I am crazy for Sweetwood beef jerky, which is just perfect for my carnivore needs. I mean, I'm not that far from my wolf days and eating these hunks of meat makes me feel so alive and wild.

Do you like being an only pet?

I really love being the center of attention. I already struggle enough with having to share my mom's attention with Nelson. The guy is growing on me but it has taken some getting used to. I've been better about marking my territory in his house, which seems to make everyone happy. When my cousins Kia and Rose come around I love romping around with the big girls. There is something mysterious about those ladies. It definitely brings out the less behaved side in me, which my mom doesn't like.

"MAKE YOUR OWN PATH."

– PUPPY LALIVE

What is your favorite treat?

My favorite treat is definitely ice cream and cereal. Generally, I like most anything Nelson eats. Interestingly enough, it seems to mostly consist of ice cream and cereal! Unlike Caroline, who seems to think I might fancy some green treat that's good for my teeth. Who are you kidding?

MANGO & MELON

"LOVE YOUR FAMILY."
—MANGO & MELON SWEERS

What are your likes and dislikes?

MANGO: I like to sleep with Mom and Dad in their bed.
I hate it when my family leaves me behind.

MELON: I like food, food and more food. I also really like to roll in horse poo.

Do you like your sibling pet/ housemate?

MANGO: I love Melon (he is my son, after all), except he annoys me when he bites my ears.

What annoys you the most?

MANGO: When Melon tries to hog all the attention.

MELON: When I am sent outside just because I ate all of the pizza off the table.

MELON: I love Mango, my mom. She only sometimes gets annoyed with me.

What is your favorite memory?

MANGO: Having puppies.

MELON: Growing up with my 10 brothers and sisters.

CABOT & PICO

What are your likes and dislikes?

CABOT: I like food, running and chasing Mom's feet. I don't like getting brushed or taking a bath.

PICO: I love food, chasing my cat, being snuggled. I don't like BATHS. Which is funny because Mom owns Weavers Waggin' Wash.

What annoys you the most?

CABOT: Mom putting on my collar. PICO: Cabot.

Is there anything else you want to share with your readers?

CABOT: One week after surgery (I swallowed a whole 6" Bully Stick), I jumped out of the car window and I didn't even have any broken bones!

PICO: I am a Heeling Friends pet therapy dog and I love to cuddle with those who I visit.

"I LOVE EVERYONE AND EVERYTHING." – CABOT WEAVER

"HAPPINESS IS FINDING A BALL AND THEN KEEPING IT!" – PICO WEAVER

ZEPHYR

What is your favorite activity?

I am a very active dog and I love to be outside. In the summertime, I do my best to convince Mom to take me swimming every day. In the wintertime, I love to leap when anyone tosses or kicks snow up in the air.

What is your favorite season and why?

Summertime is my favorite because I LOVE to swim.
I swim every day for an hour while my Mom reads her book.

What do you do when you are home alone?

After ensuring that no one is home, I make the rounds and inspect every wastebasket, carefully pulling out all of the tissues and food wrappers I can find.

What annoys you the most?

A clean kitchen floor.

What is your favorite treat?

Do I have to pick only one?

MIGO

What is your favorite activity?

Swimming. That's it. Period. The end.

What do you do when you are home alone?

Nap and watch SportsCenter ...or soaps ... depending on who left the TV on.

What is your favorite season and why?

Duh...duck hunting season.

What are your dislikes?

I don't like mean dogs, going to the vet or the Comcast guy.

What is your favorite treat?

Bacon is the most delicious food in the world. Peanut Butter is a close second. #Bacon!

"WORK
IS
OVER-RATED."
—MIGO ENGESETH

101

PENNY

What is your favorite pastime?

My favorite thing to do is "sniffing," or as my kin like to say, "reading the news," only I like to getting all my news at once: online, radio, tv; newspaper and local gossip. I can tell you who, what, when and why at most bushes, trash cans and fire hydrants.

Do you like being an only pet?

Truthfully, other canines are the bane of my existence, especially the annoying ones that are always trying to herd me. I'm in charge. I know what you want to sniff. If you are going to try to herd me, watch out. I snap quick. Fortunately for me, Papa knows that and won't let Mommy burden me with an annoying housemate. I have to have 100% of the attention, which Papa and Mommy comply with. It is really the best arrangement.

CHARLIE

What is your favorite pastime?

Every morning, my mom and I have cuddle time. She rubs me on one side, she says "over" and I roll over and she rubs me on the other side. We talk about all of the things we are grateful for and she kisses me a ton!

What do you do when you are home alone?

Watch the door and wait for Mom to come home.

What is your favorite memory?

Ummm...I can't remember the question...

What is your favorite treat?

Coconut oil.

IN MEMORY OF BINGO:
THE UNCONDITIONAL LOVE OF A DOG

BY JIM STIMSON

My then-6-year-old Golden Retriever, Bingo, and I were just climbing into the car after visiting the Yampa Valley Medical Center. We were a Heeling Friends team. She was a certified Hospital Therapy Dog, a creature who found her calling in life. She was good at it and loved her work. We usually spent about an hour and a half there, two days a month, visiting patients in their rooms, as well as people waiting for tests, visitors waiting for loved ones to be released and staff.

On this day an acquaintance pulled up just as we were leaving. I knew that his father-in-law had just died so I rolled down my window, greeted him and offered condolences.

"Why are you here now?" I asked.

"It's my wife," he said. "It looks like we're going to lose her tomorrow." He was obviously shaken by the turn of events.

"We'll pay you a visit here tomorrow," I said.

The next day, Bingo and I approached the main nurse's station where we are provided with a paper, showing us which rooms are appropriate to offer to visit. Clipped to it was a note telling us to be sure to stop by a certain room. I didn't know it then, but that note was the beginning of a significant day for us. Until that day, I didn't really understand how powerful a dog could be in easing the pain and sadness of a grieving family on a dark day in their lives.

We walked by the room and it was full of people and machines, doctors and nurses doing what they could and family members watching an important member of their family slip away. Obviously, we weren't going in there. So, we visited another room, then came back by and stood to the side. One of the family members saw us. Within a few minutes all four adult children and the dad were out there, taking a much needed break from the weight of the day.

I don't know if it was my demeanor or a signal sent down the leash, but Bingo was 100 per cent aware that her very best work was needed. Nobody said a word; I'm not sure if I even made eye contact with them all. But, Bingo did. She had shelved her puppy-like silliness that she sometimes uses, and was all business as she went from person to person, sat on their feet, leaned in and solicited some pets. Pretty soon the seven of us were seated on the floor and she was going from person to person, nuzzling and rubbing against them, asking them to give back. It was nothing short of amazing to watch as the weight of the day began to lift. You could see it. Feel it. After about 10 minutes, still without a word being spoken, one by one they went back into the room. They all seemed to stand a little taller after the break with Bingo. We went on with our visits and headed for home. Bingo slept soundly all afternoon. She was tired. I saw in the paper that the woman died that afternoon.

The very next month we went back, expecting a more normal series of visits, to cheer youngsters coming out of the cloud after their tonsils were removed, or accident victims or elective surgery patients (many missing their pets) getting down to the business of recovery. But it wasn't to be.

A scenario similar to the previous month played out. This time, a woman in a hospital bed was placed at the end of the hall, and the bed was tilted so she could see the mountains to the east. The same machines and busy medical people were working. A 30-something man in a nice business suit caught my eye and whispered, "It's our mother. It's her last day." We lingered. Pretty soon four adult kids, Bingo and I were on the floor nearby and she was fully engaged once again. Again, no words, just love. Again, the weight lift was palpable. Again, when we got home, Bingo slept soundly all afternoon.

We made nearly 100 visits, twice each month. Those were our two most challenging days. Rewarding days too. Bingo loved her work. As soon as the fanny pack I wore and the credential tags we both wore came out of the closet, she didn't leave my side. She did want to miss the chance to be a Heeling Friend.

FROM "TAILS OF A PET SITTER"
BY SUE HANSEN, LEADER OF THE PACK

Blackie and Cassidy, A Love Story

Blackie, a.k.a. BD or Black Dog, was my soulmate. He was a Bearded Collie who came into my life when we both needed it most. He was a very spoiled, loved dog of my mother's. My dear mom and Blackie came to visit and help me recover from major surgery. Blackie was in dire need of exercise and I was rehabilitating from ground zero. So, as soon as I was able, Blackie and I would walk together, making daily gains of a few hundred feet. I was on crutches and he was overweight. After a month, my mom was leaving and with a tearful look, she asked if I would keep BD. He was so happy with me and getting quite fit, she knew it was the best for both of us. I could not have been happier! Black Dog had already made his way straight into my heart, riding shotgun on the middle console in the car, leaning on my right shoulder while watching where we were going. We became inseparable.

One of my concerns with BD was my pet sitting business. I take dogs into my home and care for them while their families are away. I had been doing this for over 14 years and I wasn't sure if Blackie would accept it. Since he was so intelligent, I just talked to him one night and explained that I needed him to share his home and be a good host to our visitors. Not only did he understand, but he became my best assistant ever! He greeted everyone, treated them with respect and taught them the rules. He did not like them all; he just tolerated many of them, but there were a handful that were very special.

One of those special dogs was Cassidy, a beautiful black French Standard Poodle. From the first time Cassidy was our guest, Blackie became smitten with her. He watched out for her, slept next to her, nuzzled with her and let her do things the

CASSIDY

other guests were not allowed to do. For instance, no one was allowed to sleep on the bed with me except BD. In the car, no one was allowed to ride shotgun except, you guessed it, BD.

Until Cassidy that is. Cassidy was allowed to sleep with us and take turns riding shotgun. On our group walks, Blackie was always in the front of the pack leading the way. If anyone wandered off, BD would round them up and get them back in the group. Only Cassidy was able to join him as lead dog in the front.

Cassidy was our guest several times a year. When she appeared at the door, Blackie did not do his usual "Mom, someone is at the door bark." Instead, he would start sneezing in his excitement and march with his front paws, as if he was playing a drum. She could not wait to nuzzle him and would burst through the door to greet him. Their relationship was so kind and respectful. I enjoyed it so much that many times I would purposely not schedule any other guests during the time Cassidy visited. We would take little trips together, camping and hiking in the woods.

Blackie was quite a bit older than Cassidy. As he aged and slowed down considerably, she just slowed down with him. She would not take over as lead dog; she always stayed by his side. When I had to lift BD into the car, she would patiently wait and jump in only after he was safely in the car. She was his best friend. I always wished for a relationship such as theirs. I learned so much from them.

After Blackie crossed the Rainbow Bridge, Cassidy would still come and stay with me. The first time she visited after BD died, she looked everywhere for him. I held her and told her that he had died. I showed her his collar and his bed. She knew. I left his bed out and she would sleep in it instead of her own. Then, she would join me in my bed. She always rode shotgun in the car, leaning on my right shoulder just like BD had done. I loved her as much as my Black Dog. The last time I had Cassidy as a guest, she was almost 13 years old. She couldn't see or hear anymore, but she followed me everywhere and nuzzled with me at night. A few months later, Cassidy came to me in a dream and told me she had crossed the Rainbow Bridge too. She and BD were together again and in all my sadness, I was consoled.

BLACKIE

107

ABOUT ROUTT COUNTY HUMANE SOCIETY

"The Routt County Humane Society is a non-profit organization dedicated to the prevention of cruelty to animals, providing humane education, promoting spaying and neutering as a means of decreasing the number of unwanted pets, and encouraging respect for the dignity and worth of all animals."

The Routt County Humane Society, Inc. (RCHS) is a non-profit volunteer organization that was established in 1985 by Marilyn McCaulley to serve the welfare of animals in Routt County, Colorado. It is led by an all-volunteer seven-member working Board of Directors that remains devoted to the cause of animal welfare in our community. Since its inception, RCHS has worked in conjunction with the city of Steamboat Springs to raise funds for the construction of the current animal shelter and the animal crematorium, facilitate and fund the state-required spay/neuter program, fund veterinary services, provide volunteer staffing at the shelter, provide financial assistance for pets from low income families and educate the community.

As of May 1, 2015, RCHS took over operations of the animal shelter from the city of Steamboat Springs. In addition to the services currently provided by RCHS, shelter services will expand to include behavioral training for animals and added staff members with expanded hours. Having RCHS take over the animal shelter provides benefits to the city, the Humane Society and the community. With RCHS at the helm, the Humane Society will be able to secure grant funding more easily, increase the staff, increase existing services and start new volunteer programs, implement new dog training programs and have more general control over shelter operations. RCHS also envisions purchasing new equipment and securing a vehicle to transport animals to and from veterinary appointments. Since taking over, the shelter has installed new shelter management software and RCHS now microchips all adopted animals. In addition, the city is funding and building a dog yard improvement project.

To accomplish the expansion of services, RCHS is initiating new fundraising campaigns. Most RCHS funds come from donors, with contributions as small as $5 or as large as $5,000. RCHS has spent many years and volunteer hours coordinating fundraisers such as dog washes, Picture Your Pet with Santa, artistic dog auctions, Artful Labs/Gimme Shelter Fundraiser, Yampa Valley Pet Calendar and Dog Kennel sponsorships. Grants have come from Lauretta Boyd Foundation, Alice Jenkins Foundation, Animal Assistance Foundation and Rainbow Bridge. In 2013, Steamboat was designated Dog Town USA by Dog Fancy Magazine, which donated $5,000 to RCHS. RCHS also recently received a $5,000 grant from Impact 100 and the Yampa Valley Community Foundation. RCHS is a recipient of the Colorado Pet Overpopulation Fund Tax Check-Off Grant Program, which provides financial assistance for 40 Routt County families to spay or neuter their pets.

Local businesses also support RCHS, including Ace Hardware, Steamboat Coffee and Tea Company, which created a "Rescue Blend" coffee with all proceeds going to RCHS, and Steamboat Snowmobile and Zipline Tours, which donated the van now used to transport shelter animals to and from their veterinary appointments. The RCHS teamed up with the Colorado DMV and now offers the opportunity to purchase an Adopt-A-Shelter-Pet license plate at our local DMV, with the proceeds going to the RCHS animal shelter.

On an individual level, many people in the community volunteer their time to organize fundraisers for RCHS. For example there is the Annual Mustache Ride every October, and in 2013 local artist MB Warner painted portraits of 60 shelter animals and sold them to raise $3000 for RCHS. Other efforts to raise money for RCHS include school projects by the Emerald Mountain School Student Council as well as several individual students and their school projects (the Citizenship Project and Bracelet Project). The Steamboat Mountain School Honor Society students also contributed by holding a talent show fundraiser for RCHS.

RCHS is diligent and proactive in finding "forever homes" for its shelter animals. In addition to newspaper advertisements listing homeless pets in need of a forever home, RCHS brings shelter animals to its booth at the Steamboat Farmers' Market throughout the summer to promote adoptions. RCHS also maintains a web page, Facebook page and a Twitter account, which all provide information about RCHS and the animals up for adoption. RCHS generates a quarterly newsletter with informational updates, volunteer needs, upcoming programs, animal health information and recognition of donors. This newsletter is found on the web site and can be downloaded or printed for easy viewing. The Dogs of Steamboat is a community Facebook page which also supports RCHS efforts to find homes for shelter dogs. In addition, RCHS has joined the Amazon Smile Program, an Amazon.com charitable program that gives shoppers the opportunity to support RCHS every time they shop, at no additional cost. Amazon will then donate 0.5% of the purchase price from an expansive list of eligible items to RCHS.

Our community is fortunate enough to have RCHS at the helm of the animal shelter. Through the diligent and compassionate efforts of the Board Members, volunteers and employees, the shelter has transformed into a sanctuary. At RCHS, each animals life matters.

PHOTOGRAPH TAKEN BY AUSTIN COLBERT AT THE ANNUAL POOCHY PADDLE, ANOTHER FUN EVENT SPONSORED BY OUR COMMUNITY TO RAISE MONEY FOR THE RCHS.

Photo by Austin Colbert

"UNTIL ONE HAS LOVED AN ANIMAL A PART OF ONE'S SOUL REMAINS UNAWAKENED."

— ANATOLE FRANCE

ABOUT THE AUTHOR

Janne Siegel is an energetic, borderline-neurotic multi-tasker. Her three dogs (her "Girls") would say she is annoyingly slow when it comes time for making dinner and going on hikes, but really nice overall, especially after she finishes her morning meditation. She practiced law for more than 20 years in her previous life and is now a writer and yoga instructor. She is writing feature books on pets, a children's book series based on animals and a pet blog. She lives in Steamboat Springs, Colorado, a.k.a. Ski Town USA and Dog Town USA, with her husband and her three patient Girls, who serve as her muses. Janne has been published in the Valley Voice and is a member of Society of Children's Books Writers and Illustrators, Rocky Mountain Chapter. When she's not writing, Janne practices and teaches yoga, loves to cook (though she's not much into grocery shopping) and pretty much participates in all activities Steamboat Springs offers each season (too many choices to list). Suffice it to say, she thoroughly embraces life in the Rocky Mountains. She believes it takes 21 days to establish a new habit, is too scared to watch a horror movie or read a horror novel, and believes in retail therapy. Visit her at her blog at deartaffy.com.

DOGS
LEAVE
PAW PRINTS
ON YOUR
HEART.

Made in the USA
Charleston, SC
23 December 2015